CONTENTS

Introduction: Good Book Guides

Every Bible-study group is different—yours may take place in a church building, in a home or in a cafe, on a train, over a leisurely mid-morning coffee or squashed into a 30-minute lunch break. Your group may include new Christians, mature Christians, non-Christians, moms and tots, students, businessmen or teens. That's why we've designed these *Good Book Guides* to be flexible for use in many different situations.

Our aim in each session is to uncover the meaning of a passage, and see how it fits into the "big picture" of the Bible. But that can never be the end. We also need to appropriately apply what we have discovered to our lives. Let's take a look at what is included:

⊕ **Talkabout:** Most groups need to "break the ice" at the beginning of a session, and here's the question that will do that. It's designed to get people talking around a subject that will be covered in the course of the Bible study.

⊕ **Investigate:** The Bible text for each session is broken up into manageable chunks, with questions that aim to help you understand what the passage is about. The **Leader's Guide** contains **guidance for questions**, and sometimes ⊗ additional "follow-up" questions.

⊕ **Explore more (optional):** These questions will help you connect what you have learned to other parts of the Bible, so you can begin to fit it all together like a jigsaw; or occasionally look at a part of the passage that's not dealt with in detail in the main study.

⊕ **Apply:** As you go through a Bible study, you'll keep coming across **apply** sections. These are questions to get the group discussing what the Bible teaching means in practice for you and, your church. ⊕ **Getting personal** is an opportunity for you to think, plan and pray about the changes that you personally may need to make as a result of what you have learned.

⊕ **Pray:** We want to encourage prayer that is rooted in God's word—in line with his concerns, purposes, and promises. So each session ends with an opportunity to review the truths and challenges highlighted by the Bible study, and turn them into prayers of request and thanksgiving.

The **Leader's Guide** and introduction provide historical background information, explanations of the Bible texts for each session, ideas for **optional extra** activities, and guidance on how best to help people uncover the truths of God's word.

In light of his return

1 & 2 Thessalonians

by Ligon Duncan

1 & 2 Thessalonians For You

If you are reading *1 & 2 Thessalonians For You* alongside this Good Book Guide, here is how the studies in this booklet link to the chapters of *1 & 2 Thessalonians For You*:

Study One → Ch 1-2 Study Five → Ch 8-10
Study Two → Ch 3-4 Study Six → Ch 11
Study Three → Ch 5 Study Seven → Ch 12-13
Study Four → Ch 6-7 Study Eight → Ch 14

Find out more about *1 & 2 Thessalonians For You* at:
www.thegoodbook.com/for-you

In Light of His Return
The Good Book Guide to 1 & 2 Thessalonians
© Ligon Duncan/The Good Book Company, 2023.
Series Consultants: Tim Chester, Tim Thornborough,
Anne Woodcock, Carl Laferton

Published by:
The Good Book Company

thegoodbook.com | thegoodbook.co.uk
thegoodbook.com.au | thegoodbook.co.nz | thegoodbook.co.in

Published in association with the literary agency of Wolgemuth & Associates.

ISBN: 9781784985042 | JOB-007313 | Printed in Turkey

Why study 1 & 2 Thessalonians?

Some people complain that Christianity is all about "pie in the sky by and by." They say we need to jettison our escapism—our thinking about heaven and the future return of Christ—in order to do a good job of living *this* life. If it's all about heaven, the charge goes, we're never going to be any earthly good.

But that charge misses the point of all the teaching in the Bible about the return of Jesus and the end of this world. Scripture is written not so that we don't care about this life but so that we live this life well—and its teaching about the future is a crucial part of that. In fact, you cannot live this life well if you're not living it in light of the second coming of Christ.

Paul's letters to the Thessalonians are two of the earliest parts of the New Testament. They were written less than 20 years after Jesus died and rose again. And they are filled with references to his second coming—since, from the earliest times, faith in Jesus would not have made sense without his return.

The letters were written to a young church plant, set up by Paul during his missionary trip to the Roman province of Macedonia (in modern-day Greece) in AD 49 or 50. Acts 17:1-10 tells us the story of how Paul preached about Jesus but was forced out of the city by those who had rejected the gospel. Paul's time with this fledgling church was short—but 1 & 2 Thessalonians show us how he continued to teach these new Christians and pray for them from afar.

In 1 Thessalonians, Paul's love for the church he had founded is on full display as he encourages these Christians to live to please God—that is, to grow in godliness: in their relationships, their work, their mourning, and their honoring of their leaders. His second letter implies that the persecution had worsened and had become unremitting; Paul explains why Christians face such suffering and how to continue in faith and love in the face of it.

In both letters, Paul links his exhortations to the coming return of the Lord Jesus. He wants the believers to endure trials and live life in light of Jesus' future coming: to stand fast in their faith in the certain hope of future glory.

These two letters open a window onto church life among the earliest Christians. But it is striking how they speak to our churches in the 21st century too. We, too, need to heed the call to remember that we are waiting for Jesus, the risen Son of God, to return from heaven. We, too, need to be exhorted to live to please God in our lives. We, too, need the gospel to shape us. Then we will become imitators of the Lord and an example to all believers (1 Thessalonians 1:6, 7).

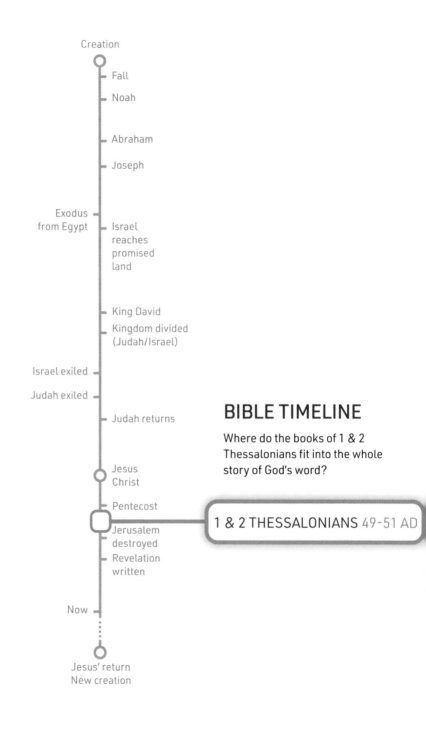

Creation

Fall

Noah

Abraham

Joseph

Exodus
from Egypt

Israel
reaches
promised
land

King David

Kingdom divided
(Judah/Israel)

Israel exiled

Judah exiled

Judah returns

BIBLE TIMELINE

Where do the books of 1 & 2
Thessalonians fit into the whole
story of God's word?

Jesus
Christ

Pentecost

1 & 2 THESSALONIANS 49-51 AD

Jerusalem
destroyed

Revelation
written

Now

Jesus' return
New creation

1 Thessalonians 1
THE WORD SOUNDED FORTH

⊕ talkabout

1. How would you describe what it means to become a Christian?

⊥ investigate

▶ Read 1 Thessalonians 1:1-10

2. Paul is writing to believers in Thessalonica—but what else (or rather, who else) are they "in" (v 1)? What do you think this means?

3. What does the Thessalonians' faith look like in their lives (v 3)?

4. These believers have become Christians fairly recently. How does Paul describe this (v 4-5)?

5. What was God's role in all of this?

explore more

optional

Paul knows that the Thessalonians are elect—chosen by God (v 4). In other words, their salvation didn't begin with them figuring something out or being a good person. It began with the love of God.

> **Read Ephesians 1:3-6**

According to these verses, when did God choose us?

What does God's choosing of us mean that we become?

Why did God do this?

How is this comforting to Christians who struggle with sin or feel they are not good enough?

Paul thanks God that when he preached the gospel in Thessalonica, it didn't just come in his words; it came with converting, saving power (1 Thessalonians 1:5). The gospel is communicated in words, but it is not just words. Through it, the Holy Spirit transforms lives.

⊟ apply

6. Think about your approach to evangelism. How might the truths we have just read impact on the way we share the gospel, the prayers we pray, and the pressure we put on ourselves?

⊡ getting personal

Is there one lesson here that particularly impacts you personally? Perhaps it's a truth you hadn't thought about before or a helpful correction to your attitude toward evangelism. You might find it helpful to write it down to help you remember it.

↑ pray

Share about one person each with whom you would like to share the gospel, and pause to pray together for those people.

↓ investigate

Wherever the gospel is accepted, the Holy Spirit is at work. He comes to convert, and he comes to sanctify. Paul next tells us more about how the Spirit was at work in Thessalonica.

7. What have the Thessalonian believers done, and what impact has this had (v 6-10)?

8. What kind of example do you think your church sets to other believers?

9. What does verse 6 tell us about what the Christian life is like?

10. What specific new beliefs have the Thessalonians embraced (v 9-10)?

⊡ getting personal

The Thessalonians were worshipers of pagan idols. But their story is our story too. All of us struggle with idolatry. An idol is anything in which we think we can find ultimate security and satisfaction, instead of in God. When we became Christians, we turned away from those things; but we also have to continue to turn away from them.

Here are three questions to help you identify any idols you need to turn away from.

What do you think about when you're not thinking about anything else?

How do you spend your time, resources, and energy?

What disappoints you, or what would make you feel worthless if you lost it or failed at it?

Take some time on your own to prayerfully think through these questions. Then decide on what steps you can take to turn away from the idols you have identified!

⊟ apply

11. These beliefs clearly had a huge impact in their lives (v 3). Why does each of these beliefs transform us?

12. The Thessalonian Christians made the gospel visible: in other words, their lives displayed the fact that the gospel is real and true. In what ways can this also be true of us today?

⊡ pray

Pray for one another in the light of your answers to questions 11 and 12.

2

1 Thessalonians 2
A MANNER WORTHY OF GOD

The story so far

Paul began with thankfulness for all that God had done in the Thessalonian Christians—showing us what it looks like to be transformed by the gospel.

⊕ talkabout

1. What does it mean to live in a way that is "worthy" of someone?

⊥ investigate

In 1 Thessalonians 2 – 3, Paul is defending his ministry to the Thessalonian church. It seems there are people in Thessalonica who are trying to undermine his credibility. So Paul recounts, describes, and explains what he did when he was in Thessalonica. As he does, we learn what it looks like to live to please God, even amid opposition.

> ▸ **Read 1 Thessalonians 2:1-8**

2. According to verses 2-4, what was Paul's mission in Thessalonica, and what was his motivation?

DICTIONARY

Philippi (v 2): a city in Greece.
Pretext (v 5): excuse.
Apostles (v 6): those specifically sent out by the risen Christ.

3. What does this mean Paul *didn't* do (v 5-6)?

4. How did he treat the new believers (v 7-8)?

• Think about the "nursing mother" idea. What does a breastfeeding mother do? What does this imply about Paul's attitude and behavior?

5. How does this help us to understand what it means "not to please man, but to please God" (v 4)?

⊡ **getting personal**

What about you? Do you ever get trapped into seeking to please people over and above pleasing God? How does this manifest itself in your life? What steps could you take to remind yourself to please God first and foremost?

⊟ apply

6. Can you think of some situations when people (even Christians) might be tempted to do the things Paul outlines in verses 5-6?

• How can we instead put into practice the boldness, gentleness, and commitment he describes in verses 2, 7, and 8?

⬆ pray

Pause to pray for one another in the light of what you've discussed so far.

⬇ investigate

▶ **Read 1 Thessalonians 2:9-20**

7. What three aspects of his ministry does Paul highlight in verses 9-12?

• Verse 9

DICTIONARY

Exhorted (v 12): encouraged, instructed.
Charged (v 12): urged, instructed.
Gentiles (v 16): non-Jewish people.
Hindering (v 16): preventing.

• Verse 10

• Verses 11-12

8. What was the point of all of Paul's ministry (v 12)?

9. What do verses 13-16 show us about what it means to walk in a manner worthy of God?

• What do these verses show us about what it means to displease God?

⊡ explore more

Very sadly, 1 Thessalonians 2:14-16 has sometimes been interpreted as anti-Semitic. Anti-Semitism means suspicion, hatred, or discrimination toward Jewish people simply because of their ethnicity. It is a very, very serious charge. We need to be totally clear that biblical Christianity emphatically rejects anti-Semitism and holds it to be a grave sin.

▶ Read Romans 9:1-5

Paul's "brothers" in verse 3 are Jewish people. What was Paul's attitude toward them?

This passage in 1 Thessalonians is not talking about all Jews, as if to be Jewish is to be sinful. Paul is observing the terrible things that were done by certain Jews.

In verse 14 we see that the Thessalonians have suffered as much from Gentiles as the Jewish Christians in Judea have suffered from the Jews. Both Gentiles and Jews have persecuted God's people. It's also true that both Gentiles and Jews have come into God's people through faith in Christ.

10. Based on verses 17-20, what do you think people might have been saying about Paul? What's the truth?

⊖ apply

11. Look back over the whole of 1 Thessalonians 2. What difference would you say it makes to our lives when we live to please God?

12. How can we put those things into practice today?

⊞ **pray**

Share about some specific ways in which you are thankful for God's work in people you know. Then share about some Christian individuals and groups you know of who are facing suffering, isolation, or opposition, as Paul and the Thessalonian Christians did. Thank God for his call on these people's lives and ask him to help them walk in a manner worthy of him.

3

1 Thessalonians 3

GOOD NEWS OF YOUR FAITH

The story so far

Paul began with thankfulness for all that God had done in the Thessalonian Christians—showing us what it looks like to be transformed by the gospel.

We then heard about Paul's own ministry among the Thessalonians and saw what it means to live to please God, even amid opposition.

⊕ talkabout

1. What is some good news you have received recently?

⬇ investigate

At the end of chapter 2, Paul explained that he had tried to come back to the Thessalonians but couldn't. In chapter 3 he tells us the solution he found—and it's good news!

> **Read 1 Thessalonians 3:1-8**

2. What did Paul do, and what was his purpose in this (v 1-2)?

DICTIONARY

Moved (v 3): Paul means disturbed or upset.
The tempter (v 5): the devil.
Fast (v 8): fixed, firm.

3. What does Paul want the Thessalonians to know about the afflictions he is experiencing (v 3-4)?

- Why might hearing about these afflictions have affected the Thessalonians' faith?

⌨ **getting personal**

When you're going through a difficult time, how do you tend to talk about it to others?

It's good to be honest about what we're feeling, but it's also important to seek to build others up—to consider the impact of our words on those we're talking to. Thinking about others can also help us to have a different perspective on our sufferings, as we see in verse 7.

Reread verses 1-8 and ask God to help you have a perspective like Paul's when you are experiencing afflictions.

4. What news has Timothy brought (v 6)?

5. Why do you think this news affected Paul so strongly (v 7-8)?

⊡ **explore more**

optional

⊡ **explore more**

To understand Paul's feelings on this more fully, we can look back at the end of chapter 2.

▶ **Read 1 Thessalonians 2:19-20**

How does Paul describe the Thessalonians here?

Paul is saying, *You want to know what I'm in it for? I'm in it for the day when I hand you over to Jesus and you're safe home for eternity.* That's the reward he wants; that's the best thing he can achieve with his life.

⊟ **apply**

6. Paul's dearest concern is that the believers will stand firm in their faith. If that were our dearest concern too, how would it affect…

   • what we say to each other?

   • what we invest time and energy in?

⬆ **pray**

Pause to ask God for his help in putting your answers to question 6 into practice.

⊌ investigate

> ▶ **Read 1 Thessalonians 3:9-13**

DICTIONARY

Abound in (v 12): have lots of.
Saints (v 13): Christians.

7. What do you think is the tone of these verses overall?

8. How does Paul express his joy in verses 9-10?

9. What does Paul continue to pray for (v 10-13)?

10. By "what is lacking in your faith" (v 10), Paul means teaching about the gospel. How do you think this links to the love and holiness Paul talks about in verses 12-13?

11. What is Paul ultimately looking forward to?

Paul does not just want the Thessalonians to grow in love or become a bit more holy. He wants them to "abound in love" and be completely "blameless."

How does this challenge you? Are there areas of your life where God may be particularly calling you to abound in love or be blameless in holiness?

⊡ **apply**

12. Can you think of specific individuals for whom you can pray some or all of Paul's words in verses 9-13?

⊡ **pray**

Write down some short prayers for specific people based on what you've read. Pray them together now and then take them away to keep on praying them throughout the week.

4 1 Thessalonians 4
MORE AND MORE

The story so far

Paul gave thanks for the transforming work of God in the Thessalonians' lives. He recalled his time with them, showing what it means to live to please God.

Although Paul was kept from visiting the Thessalonians again, he was comforted by Timothy's news that they were standing firm in their faith.

⊕ talkabout

1. What techniques do people use to get others to behave in a certain way? Which techniques do you think are most effective?

⤓ investigate

Paul has already said he wants the Thessalonians to "walk in a manner worthy of God" (1 Thessalonians 2:12). Now he gets specific.

▶ Read 1 Thessalonians 4:1-12

2. What is Paul's tone as he starts his instructions (v 1)?

> **DICTIONARY**
>
> **Sanctification (v 3):** becoming more godly.
> **Abstain (v 3):** to not do something.
> **Transgress (v 6):** sin.

3. Paul's first set of instructions is about sexual immorality. What are the three points he makes in verses 3-6?

• How do verses 3-8 help us to understand what sexual immorality is and why it is serious?

optional

⊡ explore more

What does Paul mean when he says that sexual sin wrongs our brothers and sisters in Christ? There are some examples where the answer is obvious: an adulterous husband sins against his wife; a person watching porn is complicit in the exploitation rife in that industry. But Paul's meaning is wider than that. When we are immoral, we are sinning against our brothers and sisters in Christ in any and every instance.

❯ Read Romans 12:4-5 and 1 Corinthians 6:17-20

What do these passages tell us about our relationship with each other and our relationship with Christ?

According to 1 Corinthians 6, why is sexual immorality sinning against God?

Given what we saw in Romans 12, why is sexual immorality therefore sinning against our brothers and sisters?

4. Paul says that knowing God makes Christians more able to control their bodies than the Gentiles (v 4-5). What does Paul say about God that helps and motivates us (v 3, 6, 7-8)?

5. What observations does Paul make about the believers' love for one another in verses 9-10?

6. Why does Paul give the instructions in verse 11? What do you think each of them means?

⊡ apply

7. Overall in this passage, what kind of people does Paul want us to become? Practically, what can we do to become more like this?

⊡ pray

Spend a moment praying for one another in the light of what you've read. Before you pray, you might want to share one or two ways each in which you would like to grow in godliness.

⊡ investigate

Paul's aim in this letter is to teach Christians how to live life in light of Jesus' return. The instructions in the first half of chapter 4 have focused on life now. The remaining verses explore what's going to happen in the future.

▶ Read 1 Thessalonians 4:13-18

8. What is the practical purpose of what Paul writes here (v 13)?

DICTIONARY
Precede (v 15): come before.

The Thessalonians know that Jesus will come again, but they seem to be worrying about what happens to believers who die before that happens (that is what Paul means by "those who are asleep", v 13).

9. What are the two key truths in verse 14 that bring us hope?

• Why is Paul so confident of these truths (v 15)?

10. Use the following questions to help you trace out the various steps Paul describes in verses 16-17.

• What will Jesus do (v 16)?

• Who will rise first (v 16)?

• What will happen next (v 17)?

• What is the eternal future we're looking forward to (v 17)?

11. Why do you think these things should encourage us (v 18)?

⊡ getting personal

Who do you know who needs comfort and encouragement right now—perhaps because they are grieving or perhaps for another reason? What could you do or say to encourage them this week?

⊟ apply

12. How do you think it changes our approach to life now if we believe these truths about the future?

⬆ pray

Spend time reflecting on the future God has promised us and asking for God's help in living life in light of that future. You might find it helpful to sing (or just listen to) a song together—for example, "Christ Our Hope in Life and Death" by Jordan Kauflin, Keith Getty, and Matt Boswell (Getty Music Publishing).

5

1 Thessalonians 5
CHILDREN OF LIGHT

The story so far

Paul thanked God for his transforming work in the Thessalonians' lives. He recalled his visit to them and said he'd been comforted by reports of their faith.

He then urged them to live to please God, instructing them to abstain from sexual immorality, love one another, and look forward to Jesus' return.

⊕ talkabout

1. What do people today think might bring about the end of the world as we know it? When people believe these things, how does it affect the way they live now?

⊥ investigate

1 Thessalonians 5 is where Paul begins to tackle his key theme of the return of Christ head-on.

❯ Read 1 Thessalonians 5:1-11

2. Why doesn't Paul need to write about the "times and seasons" of Jesus' return (v 1-2)?

DICTIONARY

The day of the Lord (v 2): the day when Jesus returns.

3. What do you think the metaphor about labor pains tells us about the day of Jesus' return?

4. We can't know when it will happen—but Paul says that it doesn't have to be an unpleasant surprise (v 4). What is it that means we can be safe when Jesus returns (v 5, 8-10)?

When Paul uses the word "darkness" here, he means spiritual and moral darkness—sin and ignorance about God. What Paul says about being awake and sober follows on from this. The point isn't really about not getting drunk. Paul is telling us to live in a way that is in line with the light (the truth about God), not in a way that is in line with the darkness (ignorance of God).

5. What are Paul's specific instructions (v 6-11)?

→ apply

6. In what areas of life is it tempting to lack self-control and therefore live in line with the darkness?

- How can we "encourage one another and build one another up" in these situations?

⊡ getting personal

What is one thing you personally can do to build someone up in faith this week—perhaps someone you live with?

⊤ pray

"God has not destined us for wrath, but to obtain salvation through our Lord Jesus Christ, who died for us so that whether we are awake or asleep we might live with him." (1 Thessalonians 5:9-10)

Spend some time praising God for his amazing grace and praying for one another in the light of that.

⊥ investigate

Paul now offers some concluding words on how we are to pursue godliness as a church.

❯ Read 1 Thessalonians 5:12-28

7. How would you sum up the attitude Paul wants us to have to each other (v 12-15)?

DICTIONARY

Admonish (v 12): teach or warn.
Quench (v 19): literally this word means to put out a fire.
Sanctify you (v 22): make you holy.

8. How would you sum up Paul's big prayer for the Thessalonians (v 23-24)?

9. What role does each of the following people play in the sanctification of the believers?

• Church leaders (v 12)

• All Christians in a church (v 13-15)

• God himself (v 19-20, 24)

⠢ explore more

optional

In verses 19-21 Paul is clearly speaking of extraordinary prophetic activity. In New Testament times there were genuine prophets who could proclaim the revelation of God. But there were also those who peddled lies. Paul is telling the Thessalonians to take prophecy seriously (not to "quench the Spirit")—but to test what they hear.

▶ Read Acts 17:10-11

How did the Bereans test Paul's prophetic words?

Commentators disagree on what exactly "prophecies" means in 1 Thessalonians 5 and whether God speaks afresh in our day in the same way. But these verses still apply to us. "Do not quench the Spirit" (v 19) just means "Don't resist the Spirit's work".

▶ Read Acts 24:24-25

In what sense do you think Felix was quenching the Spirit?

How might we do something similar today, even as Christians?

⊡ **getting personal**

Who would you say has played a role in your own sanctification? In what way did they help you grow? Have you ever thanked them? What could you do to play a similar role in someone else's life?

10. Look at the commands in verses 16-22. How might each of these help us to live in the light of Jesus' return?

11. How does Paul's prayer in verses 23-24 help us as we seek to grow in godliness?

⊡ **apply**

12. Which of the various commands here do you think your church or your group could particularly grow in?

↥ **pray**

Spend some time praying for your church and for one another in the light of what you've read. You could finish with Paul's prayer in verses 23-24.

2 Thessalonians 1
FAITH IN AFFLICTION

The story so far

Paul thanked God for his transforming work in the Thessalonians' lives. He recalled his visit to them and said he'd been comforted by reports of their faith.

He then urged them to live to please God, instructing them to abstain from sexual immorality, love one another, and look forward to Jesus' return.

Paul ended his first letter by talking more about what it means to live in light of Jesus' second coming, with some final instructions and prayers.

⊕ talkabout

1. Can you think of some times when people have opposed your faith? What happened? How did you respond?

⊥ investigate

> **Read 2 Thessalonians 1:1-12**

2. Why do you think Paul starts with thanksgiving (v 3-4)?

DICTIONARY

Righteous (v 5): just and right.
Resolve (v 11): determination to do something.

3. What is currently happening to the Thessalonians, and how are they responding (v 4)?

Paul says that this situation is "evidence of the righteous judgment of God." But why?

4. One reason is given in verse 5. What does this situation tell us about the Thessalonian Christians? (See also verse 4.)

• Why might suffering actually be a good thing for them, therefore?

⊡ explore more

When might suffering be a good thing? Here are some other New Testament examples that shed light on this idea.

▶ Read Acts 5:41 and Philippians 1:29

What view of persecution is given here? How does this contrast with our usual view of suffering?

▶ Read 1 Peter 1:6-7

What is good about suffering in this instance?

This is a great challenge to us!

5. Another reason why persecution is evidence of God's righteous judgment is given in verses 6-10. What does Paul tell us about the persecutors (v 6, 8)?

• Why is God right to punish them, therefore?

These afflictions show that God's final judgment is just. Some people don't like the doctrine of God's final judgment. They say it's unfair; God ought to forgive everybody. But when we see someone being mistreated, we rightly want the wrongdoers to be punished! So the afflictions that the Thessalonians are enduring are evidence that God is right to punish sinners—they are "evidence of the righteous judgment of God."

At the same time, the Christians' faithful response to suffering proves the reality of their faith. They have really been saved—they have really made Jesus the Lord of their lives—and so God is just when he forgives them for their sin. Once again, this situation is "evidence of the righteous judgment of God."

→ **apply**

6. How might this understanding of God's righteous judgment influence the way we respond to unjust and sinful behavior?

• What do verses 3-4 suggest we could pray in response to suffering?

⬆ pray

Use some of the words from verses 3-4 to pray for those you know who are suffering at the moment.

⬇ investigate

7. What does Paul say will happen to the persecutors when Jesus returns (v 8-9)?

8. What's the key thing the persecutors will miss out on (v 9)?

9. What does Paul say will happen to those who have been persecuted, meanwhile (v 7, 10)—and what qualifies them for this?

10. How does this illustrate what we have seen already about how God distinguishes between people to punish and people to save?

➡️ apply

11. How does this passage encourage us to stick to our resolve when we encounter those who oppose the gospel?

12. How might praying a prayer like the one mentioned in verses 11-12 help us to be confident as we face suffering?

⬆ pray

Use some of the words from Paul's description of his prayer in verses 11-12 to give thanks to God and pray for one another.

LET NO ONE DECEIVE YOU

The story so far

The Thessalonians were facing persecution, but Paul encouraged them to see that this was evidence of God's righteous judgment—we can trust him!

⊕ talkabout

1. Can you think of some things that might shake people's faith, causing them to doubt or to disobey God?

⊕ investigate

▶ **Read 2 Thessalonians 2:1-12**

2. Why is Paul writing this passage (v 1-2)?

> **DICTIONARY**
>
> **Exalts himself (v 4):** lifts himself up.
> **Perishing (v 10):** dying.

In verse 3 Paul mentions the "man of lawlessness," who will appear before Jesus returns. Scholars are not sure exactly who this figure is. But let's look at what Paul spells out for us about him.

3. What does he do (v 4)?

• What is going to happen to him (v 8)?

• What's happening to him right now (v 6)?

• Who sends him (v 9)?

⊡ **explore more**

optional

Here is an important thing to note about this figure: he is a "son of destruction" (v 3). Jesus used this same phrase to talk about Judas Iscariot in John 17:12. Judas' sin was to betray and work against Jesus—and as a result he lost his own life. This new son of destruction will do the same thing. "Son of destruction" means not just someone who brings destruction but who will themselves be destroyed. So this "man of lawlessness" is no real threat to God's sovereign plan.

The book of Daniel includes several prophecies that may refer to the same figure.

▶ **Read Daniel 8:24-25**

What points of similarity can you spot with the passage in 2 Thessalonians?

Why is this passage ultimately one of comfort?

4. Many people will be deluded by this "man of lawlessness." Who are these people—what have they already done (v 10, 12)?

• How do they come to be deluded (v 10-12)?

5. How can we avoid being deluded or deceived ourselves, therefore?

Paul says he is writing to prevent his readers from becoming alarmed (v 2). Reading about the mysterious "man of lawlessness" might make us feel more alarmed, not less! But we don't need to be. Paul is clear that although Satan seeks to deceive us, God is always in control. We know Satan's plans ahead of time. We can avoid being taken in by him simply by loving the truth that has already been revealed to us.

⤵ **apply**

6. How do we do this? What does it look like in our daily lives to love the truth?

7. All of this doesn't just apply to the end times. In what ways might we be tempted to worship the wrong thing or give in to Satan's deceptions? How can we stand against this?

⊡ **getting personal**

How does this apply to you personally? What threatens to shake your faith?

⬆ **pray**

Take a moment to reflect quietly on what you've read and discussed. Ask God to give you confidence and not fear.

⬇ **investigate**

▶ **Read 2 Thessalonians 2:13-17**

8. In verses 13-14 Paul reminds his readers of several things which are true of all believers. What are they?

DICTIONARY

Firstfruits (v 13): the earliest part of a crop.

9. In the light of what we read in verses 1-12, why do these truths give us comfort and hope?

10. Why do you think this chapter closes with Paul writing a prayer of benediction (v 16-17)?

11. How does the past inform what Paul prays for the future here?

→ **apply**

12. Why might verses 13-17 be helpful for someone who is…

• afraid about something in the future or something happening now?

• doubtful and uneasy about the end times?

• being attracted by false teaching?

pray

Take time to write out verses 16-17 on some paper which you could use as a bookmark. As you do, reflect on some situations that might make you afraid or shake you, and consider the truths you have learned about.

Praise God together for his glorious truth, and pray for one another or for others you know who are either fearful and shaken or starting to be attracted by lies and delusions.

Keep your bookmark safe and continue to pray this prayer for yourself and others throughout the week.

8

2 Thessalonians 3
DO NOT GROW WEARY

The story so far

The Thessalonians were facing persecution, but Paul encouraged them to see that this was evidence of God's righteous judgment—we can trust him!

Paul then told his readers that the "man of lawlessness" would come—but Jesus will destroy him. We need to stand firm in the truth and not be deceived.

⊕ talkabout

1. What things might give people either confidence or a lack of confidence in how to pray for others?

⊥ investigate

▶ **Read 2 Thessalonians 3:1-5**

2. What does Paul ask for prayer for (v 1-2)?

DICTIONARY

Delivered (v 2): rescued.
Steadfastness (v 5): total, steady trustworthiness and consistency.

3. What does he suggest *he* is praying for (v 5)?

4. How does Paul show his confidence in God throughout these verses—despite the opposition?

5. Why will focusing on the love of God and the steadfastness of Christ help the Thessalonians (and us) to have confidence too?

⊡ **apply**

6. Who could you pray both of these things for?

⊡ **pray**

Take a moment to turn your discussion from question 6 into prayer.

getting personal

How do you think the Thessalonian Christians felt when they read this paragraph? I imagine they were hugely encouraged—both to hear about Paul's confidence in God and to know what he was praying for them.

Is there someone you could encourage this week in a similar way? You could send them a message with a written-out prayer you've been praying for them. Or simply seek to remind someone of how amazing God is.

investigate

Paul is not quite finished. It's as if he has read back through the letter and thought of a few more instructions he wants to add!

Read 2 Thessalonians 3:6-18

DICTIONARY

Idleness (v 6): laziness.
In accord with (v 6): consistently with.

7. What behavior has Paul heard about in the Thessalonian church (v 6, 10-11)?

- How does this contrast with Paul's own attitude to work (v 7-8)?

It seems likely that this idleness has arisen from a wrong understanding of Jesus' return. Some of the believers think he will come back immediately, and so conclude that there's no point in earning their living.

8. But what does Paul say they ought to be doing and why?

9. Why might the idleness of some believers have caused others to "grow weary in doing good" (v 13)?

⊡ explore more

optional

Paul is not telling us that we should never be dependent on one another. The New Testament clearly shows us that we should look after those who are vulnerable and unable to work. Paul's instructions here refer to those who are simply unwilling to work—and are taking advantage of others.

❯ Read 1 Corinthians 12:21-27

Here Paul is comparing the church to a body and Christians to body parts.

What point about our relationship to each other does this metaphor help us to grasp (v 25-26)?

Why does idleness threaten our relationships as Christians?

Why does a lack of generosity to each other also threaten our relationships as Christians?

10. What attitude does Paul want Christians to have toward believers who are being disobedient (v 14-15)?

⊡ **getting personal**

How does this passage challenge you personally? Perhaps you are sliding into disobedience and not taking your own sin seriously enough. Perhaps you are seeing others disobey and are starting to grow weary of remaining obedient. Perhaps you are tempted to condone or ignore wrongdoing among other believers. Perhaps you have been too harsh toward fellow Christians who have gone wrong. What needs to change?

11. Paul prays for God's peace "at all times in every way" (v 16). What kinds of peace might this congregation need?

⤷ **apply**

12. How does this chapter as a whole help us to understand what it should look like to be the church?

⬆ **pray**

Pray for your church in the light of this passage. Pray for peace, unity, righteousness, and a heart for mission. Pray that God may "direct your hearts to the love of God and to the steadfastness of Christ" (v 5).

In light of his return

return

LEADER'S GUIDE

Leader's Guide

INTRODUCTION

Leading a Bible study can be a bit like herding cats—everyone has a different idea of what the passage could be about, and a different line of enquiry that they want to pursue. But a good group leader is more than someone who just referees this kind of discussion. You will want to:

- correctly understand and handle the Bible passage. But also...

- encourage and train the people in your group to do this for themselves. Don't fall into the trap of spoon-feeding people by simply passing on the information in the Leader's Guide. Then...

- make sure that no Bible study is finished without everyone knowing how the passage is relevant for them. What changes do you all need to make in the light of the things you have been learning? And finally...

- encourage the group to turn all that has been learned and discussed into prayer.

Your Bible-study group is unique, and you are likely to know better than anyone the capabilities, backgrounds, and circumstances of the people you are leading. That's why we've designed these guides with a number of optional features. If they're a quiet bunch, you might want to spend longer on *talkabout*. If your time is limited, you can choose to skip *explore more*, or get people to look at these questions at home. Can't get enough of Bible study? Well, some studies have optional extra homework projects. As leader, you can adapt and select the material to the needs of your particular group.

So what's in the Leader's Guide?

The main thing that this Leader's Guide will help you to do is to understand the major teaching points in the passage you are studying, and how to apply them. As well as guidance for the questions, the Leader's Guide for each session contains the following important sections:

THE BIG IDEA

One or two key sentences will give you the main point of the session. This is what you should be aiming to have fixed in people's minds as they leave the Bible study. And it's the point you need to head back toward when the discussion goes off at a tangent.

SUMMARY

An overview of the passage, including plenty of useful historical background information.

OPTIONAL EXTRA

Usually this is an introductory activity that ties in with the main theme of the Bible study, and is designed to "break the ice" at the beginning of a session. Or it may be a "homework project" that people can tackle during the week.

So let's take a look at the various different features of a Good Book Guide:

⊕ talkabout

Each session kicks off with a discussion question, based on the group's opinions or experiences. It's designed to get people talking and thinking in a general way about the main subject of the Bible study.

⬇ investigate

The first thing you and your group need to know is what the Bible passage is about, which is the purpose of these questions. But watch out—people may come up with answers based on their experiences or teaching they have heard in the past, without referring to the passage at all. It's amazing how often we can get through a Bible study without actually looking at the Bible! If you're stuck for an answer, the Leader's Guide contains guidance for questions. These are the answers to direct your group to. This information isn't meant to be read out to people—ideally, you want them to discover these answers from the Bible for themselves. Sometimes there are optional follow-up questions (see ⊻ in guidance for questions) to help you help your group get to the answer.

⊡ explore more

These questions generally point people to other relevant parts of the Bible. They are useful for helping your group to see how the passage fits into the "big picture" of the whole Bible. These sections are OPTIONAL—only use them if you have time. Remember that it's better to finish in good time having really grasped one big thing from the passage, than to try and cram everything in.

⊟ apply

We want to encourage you to spend more time working at application—too often, it is simply tacked on at the end. In the Good Book Guides, apply sections are mixed in with the investigate sections of the study. We hope that people will realize that application is not just an optional extra, but rather, the whole purpose of studying the

Bible. We do Bible study so that our lives can be changed by what we hear from God's word. If you skip the application, the Bible study hasn't achieved its purpose.

These questions draw out practical lessons that we can all learn from the Bible passage. You can review what has been learned so far, and think about practical differences that this should make in our churches and our lives. The group gets the opportunity to talk about what they personally have learned.

⊡ getting personal

These can be done at home, but it is well worth allowing a few moments of quiet reflection during the study for each person to think and pray about specific changes they need to make in their own lives. Why not have a time for reporting back at the beginning of the following session, so that everyone can be encouraged and challenged by one another to make application a priority?

⬆ pray

In Acts 4:25-30 the first Christians quoted Psalm 2 as they prayed in response to the persecution of the apostles by the Jewish religious leaders. Today however, it's not as common for Christians to base prayers on the truths of God's word as it once was. As a result, our prayers tend to be weak, superficial, and self-centered rather than bold, visionary, and God-centered.

The prayer section is based on what has been learned from the Bible passage. How different our prayer times would be if we were genuinely responding to what God has said to us through his word.

1 Thessalonians 1

THE WORD SOUNDED FORTH

THE BIG IDEA

The message of the gospel changes lives. Let's live in a way that makes the gospel visible.

SUMMARY

Paul begins his letter by describing how the Thessalonian believers became Christians. In his very first greeting, he reminds them that they are "in" God—united to the Lord (v 1). That's their identity now that they have received Christ. Paul then describes what the Thessalonians' faith looks like (v 3) and describes how they came to have it, emphasizing the fact that God loved and chose them (v 4-5). Paul thanks God that when he preached the gospel in Thessalonica, it didn't just come in his words; it came with saving power as the Holy Spirit transformed lives.

Paul then speaks more about how the Holy Spirit has been at work in Thessalonica. Because these believers have joyfully received and obeyed the word, they have earned a godly reputation, with the result that other Christians have heard about it and want to be like them (v 6-8).

The first chapter closes with a description of what it means to come to faith (v 9-10). The Thessalonians turned from idols, served God, and believed that Jesus had saved them and would come again. It is these beliefs that the Thessalonians are making visible in their lives.

OPTIONAL EXTRA

This passage talks about the word of God going forth not only through literal words but also through actions. Here is a game to illustrate that. Every group member must write down a famous name and put it in a hat. Then pass the hat around. The first person to play should draw out a name and describes the person until the group guesses who it is—then keeps going with further names until 30 seconds have elapsed, scoring one point for each name guessed within the time. Once everyone has had a go, put the names back in the hat and repeat; but this time only actions can be used—no speaking! It's a fun game and a useful illustration of how actions and words often work best together.

GUIDANCE FOR QUESTIONS

1. How would you describe what it means to become a Christian? To get discussion going, you could ask group members what they experienced when they became a Christian—how it felt, what they were thinking about, how their life changed, and so on. This question is designed to warm the group up ready to look at how Paul describes what happened to the Thessalonian Christians when they came to faith.

2. Paul is writing to believers in Thessalonica—but what else (or rather, who else) are they "in" (v 1)? What do you think this means? This is a life-defining greeting. Paul is reminding his readers that they are united to God. They're under his protection. That's who they are!

3. What does the Thessalonians' faith look like in their lives (v 3)? Paul talks about their "work of faith and labor of love and steadfastness of hope." True gospel faith results in "work"—the work of caring for one another and for the needy and of sharing the gospel. This work is a "labor of love." Labor means toil; this is hard work. But it is motivated by the love of God. They also show steadfastness and perseverance because they have hope—hope in Jesus' return.

4. These believers have become Christians fairly recently. How does Paul describe this (v 4-5)?
- They have been chosen by God (v 4).
- The gospel came to them in words (v 5).
- The gospel came to them with power in the Holy Spirit (v 5).
- This resulted in "full conviction" (v 5).

5. What was God's role in all of this? God was responsible for the Thessalonians' salvation from start to finish. He chose them before the beginning of the world (see Explore More below); he spoke his word and empowered it by his Holy Spirit.

EXPLORE MORE
Read Ephesians 1:3-6
According to these verses, when did God choose us? Before the foundation of the world.
What does God's choosing of us mean that we become?
- v 4: We become holy and blameless before him.
- v 5: We are adopted as his sons.
Why did God do this? Verse 6 says it is all "to the praise of his glorious grace." God set his love on us even though we did not deserve it, to show how wonderful his love is.
How is this comforting to Christians who struggle with sin or feel they **are not good enough?** God's electing love relies on nothing that we are or do, and therefore we cannot lose it through anything that we are or do. We are unconditionally loved!

6. APPLY: Think about your approach to evangelism. How might the truths we have just read impact on the way we share the gospel, the prayers we pray, and the pressure we put on ourselves?
- We need words. Some people say that it is enough to live in a way that reflects the gospel. Of course, we must practice what we preach. But we do also need to share the truth about Jesus in words.
- We need God's power. Our words cannot save; only God can. We should pray for his power to come upon the unbelievers we are talking to "with full conviction."
- We need to remember that this is God's work. The Thessalonians didn't become Christians because of their own good works or their own interest in Jesus. They became Christians because God set his love on them. This can empower our prayers; instead of hoping that our friend will work out the truth on their own, we can pray that God will reveal it to them and that it will prove to be the case that they are among those whom he has chosen since the beginning of the world.
- In some ways this takes the pressure off us. It's down to God, not us. But it should also be an encouragement to press on in evangelism. God uses our words to bring people to faith in a way that transforms their lives!

7. What have the Thessalonian believers done, and what impact has this had (v 6-10)? Because they have joyfully received and obeyed the word, they have earned a godly reputation among other

Christians in their own region and beyond. Just as the Thessalonian Christians wanted to be like Paul, now other Christians want to be like them.

8. What kind of example do you think your church sets to other believers? This is an open question and the answers will be specific to your church. To aid discussion, you could ask: What do people say about our church? What does our church most value or prioritize? Is there anything we could do to have more of an impact or set an even better example?

9. What does verse 6 tell us about what the Christian life is like? Christians are "imitators of … the Lord." One aspect of this is that we experience joy even in affliction, just as Jesus "for the joy that was set before him endured the cross, despising the shame" (Hebrews 12:2). Christians do not get a free pass out of affliction. But we do get a specific joy that does not wither in the soil of hardship. Whatever we lose, we cannot lose Christ, and this transforms our experience of suffering.

10. What specific new beliefs have the Thessalonians embraced (v 9-10)?
- They are worshiping the true God instead of false idols.
- They are waiting for Jesus to return from heaven.
- They believe that Jesus has been raised from the dead.
- They believe that Jesus delivers us from the wrath to come—i.e. that he has saved us from the consequences of our sin.

11. APPLY: These beliefs clearly had a huge impact in their lives (v 3). Why does each of these beliefs transform us?
- The living and true God is the one who can bring life. So believing in the living God brings us new birth and necessarily transforms us.
- Believing in Jesus' resurrection means that we have hope that we ourselves will be raised from the dead.
- Believing that Jesus has delivered us from the wrath to come means that we can look forward to eternal life rather than fearing it.
- And so confidently pursue the things of God, knowing that these things are what will last. We have hope because we know that one day we will be face to face with Jesus and can enjoy him forever.

12. APPLY: The Thessalonian Christians made the gospel visible: in other words, their lives displayed the fact that the gospel is real and true. In what ways can this also be true of us today? Like the Thessalonians, we can be…
- hard at work caring for others (v 3).
- steadfast and confident in our hope for the future (v 3, 10), not defeated by worries or despair.
- imitators of Jesus (v 6)—perhaps especially in being humble and generous.
- joyful even in affliction (v 6).

2

1 Thessalonians 2

A MANNER WORTHY OF GOD

THE BIG IDEA

When we seek to please God, it changes how we treat each other and how we respond to opposition. Let's be faithful to God and to each other.

SUMMARY

It seems there were people in Thessalonica who were trying to undermine Paul. So he defends himself by recounting how he acted when he was in Thessalonica. As he does, we learn what it looks like to live to please God.

Paul begins by recalling what he did in Thessalonica and why (v 1-12). His mission was to declare the gospel (v 2), and his motive was to please God, not to please man (v 4). This means Paul didn't use flattery, seek glory, or act out of greed (v 5-6). Rather, he loved the new believers like a mother (v 7-8). Paul recalls how hard he and his companions worked so that they wouldn't be a financial burden on the new church (v 9); how blameless their behavior was (v 10); and how fatherlike his teaching (v 11-12). Paul's desire was not only to please God himself but to teach the Thessalonians how to do likewise (v 12).

Verses 13-16 reveal that they did. They listened to the word of God and accepted it—in contrast to others who displeased God by preventing Paul and others from speaking about Jesus.

Paul closes this chapter by saying again how much he longs to see the Thessalonian church (v 17-20). "You are our glory and joy," he tells them—all because they are indeed walking in a manner worthy of God, even in the midst of opposition.

OPTIONAL EXTRA

Find some images of mothers and children to share with the group. Make sure you include newborns. You can use these to help you explore the themes raised in question 4.

GUIDANCE FOR QUESTIONS

1. What does it mean to live in a way that is "worthy" of someone? In human terms we might say that someone is or isn't worthy of another person in a romantic relationship—"He's not worthy of you," or "She's a worthy wife." It means matching up to someone: living in a way that reflects the goodness of the other person or in a way that means you deserve them. Today's passage talks about living in a way that is "worthy of God." This time it is not about being deserving—none of us deserve the relationship with God that we have been given in Christ—but about reflecting God's grace and goodness back to him.

2. According to verses 2-4, what was Paul's mission in Thessalonica, and what was his motivation? Paul had come to declare the gospel of God (v 2). His motive was to please God. Jesus had sent him to proclaim the gospel (see Acts 26:16, 18)—so Paul is obeying him. But Paul also knows that God is delighted by what he is doing. Paul longs to please his Lord.

3. What does this mean Paul *didn't* do (v 5-6)?

- Paul used no "words of flattery"—that is, he never sought to curry favor but relied on speaking the truth.
- Paul had no "pretext for greed"—that is, he never used his preaching as a cover for getting money out of people.
- Paul did not "seek glory"— that is, he never tried to be the center or the focus of his preaching but always deflected attention onto Jesus. Paul's position as an apostle was a special one, but he never abused it.

4. How did he treat the new believers (v 7-8)? Paul loved the new believers and enjoyed being with them (v 8). But more than that, he treated them the way a breastfeeding mother treats her child.

- **Think about the "nursing mother" idea. What does a breastfeeding mother do? What does this imply about Paul's attitude and behavior?** A nursing mother is one who is breastfeeding a small baby. A breastfeeding mother feeds her child every few hours—and in between, she cuddles them, plays with them, talks to them, bathes them, clothes them, and comforts them. Paul says she takes care of her own children, not leaving them to others. So this is an image of total, 24-hour commitment. Paul says "We were ready to share with you … our own selves." These new Christians were not like new employees that Paul had to train, or even new friends that he had to be kind to. They were like his children. They changed Paul's life. Paul was ready to empty himself for their sake, giving all that he had to them and putting their needs above his own.

5. How does this help us to understand what it means "not to please man, but to please God" (v 4)? When Paul says he didn't want "to please man," he does not mean that he didn't care about people. He did want to please the Thessalonians—he put their needs above his own. But this was part of his desire to please God. Paul cared about God's opinion of him first and foremost, and this meant that he was willing to say things that might be unpopular. So, this passage shows us that part of pleasing God is being faithful to him and to the truth no matter what; and another part is being faithful to those we are ministering to—just as Jesus was.

6. APPLY: Can you think of some situations when people (even Christians) might be tempted to do the things Paul outlines in verses 5-6? Encourage the group to be practical and specific here. You might discuss well-known Christian leaders who have fallen into the trap of greed or self-promotion. You might discuss your own experiences of wanting people to like you or wanting praise and affirmation and how this can muddy your motivations.

- **How can we instead put into practice the boldness, gentleness, and commitment he describes in verses 2, 7, and 8?** The first thing to discuss is how to be clear about our motives. Paul's actions were a result of his pure motive to please God. What other motives get in the way for us? Second, it will be helpful to discuss particular examples of boldness, gentleness, and commitment that group members can emulate.

7. What three aspects of his ministry does Paul highlight in verses 9-12?

- **Verse 9:** Paul worked to support himself financially so that the fledgling Christians in Thessalonica did not have to. Paul had the right to be paid for his ministry (see 1 Corinthians 9:11-14), but he did not make any such demand in Thessalonica.

- **Verse 10:** Paul's behavior was above reproach. Of course, he was not without sin. But he knows that in these matters he was living as God would have him live.

- **Verses 11-12:** Paul compares himself to a father exhorting and encouraging his children. Like a good father, Paul was committed to the believers' good and was tireless in teaching them.

8. What was the point of all of Paul's ministry (v 12)? He wanted the believers to walk in a manner worthy of God. In other words, he wanted them to know the God who had called them and to live in a way that pleased him.

9. What do verses 13-16 show us about what it means to walk in a manner worthy of God?
- Listening to God's word and taking it seriously—recognizing that it is the word of God and inviting God to work in us through it (v 13).
- Imitating other faithful Christians (v 14).
- Being willing to suffer for Christ and still believing in him and in the gospel (v 14).

- **What do these verses show us about what it means to displease God?** Paul says that the Jews he knew in Judea were displeasing God "by hindering us from speaking to the Gentiles that they might be saved" (v 16). They were sinful already—rejecting God's rule—but preventing others from hearing the good news was the finishing touch. Similarly, Paul highlights how these people were those who killed Jesus as well as other men of God. They not only had no interest in listening to God but actually took steps to prevent anyone else from listening to God either.

EXPLORE MORE
Read Romans 9:1-5
Paul's "brothers" in verse 3 are Jewish people. What was Paul's attitude toward Jewish people?
He had a deep and evident love for them.

10. Based on verses 17-20, what do you think people might have been saying about Paul? What's the truth? It seems that people were highlighting the fact that Paul had not returned to Thessalonica since his initial visit. Perhaps he didn't really care about them after all. But Paul shows that he deeply loves the Thessalonian church and wishes that he could be with them.

11. APPLY: Look back over the whole of 1 Thessalonians 2. What difference would you say it makes to our lives when we live to please God?
- It changes our attitude towards other people, bringing us together in a way nothing else can (v 7-12).
- It is demanding—Paul is ready to make big sacrifices for his fellow believers and also to bear suffering and opposition (v 1-2, 8, 14).
- It involves seeking to be righteous and blameless in our conduct (v 10).
- It means that God's word will be at work within us (v 13)—transforming us and making righteousness possible.
- It makes us bold because we have confidence in God (v 2).

12. APPLY: How can we put those things into practice today? Encourage group members to be as specific as they can.

3 1 Thessalonians 3
GOOD NEWS OF YOUR FAITH

THE BIG IDEA
The goal of ministry is to see people standing firm in their faith. Let's prioritize that in our prayers for one another.

SUMMARY
At the end of chapter 2, Paul explained that he had tried to come back to the Thessalonians but couldn't. In chapter 3 he tells us about the solution he found. He sent Timothy to strengthen and encourage the new believers in their faith (v 1-2).

Both Paul and the Thessalonians were facing "afflictions," and Paul was concerned that this might affect the believers' faith, so he wanted to assure them that suffering should not be a surprise (v 3-5); it is not outside God's plan. Thankfully, Timothy has assured Paul that the Thessalonian believers are standing firm in their faith (v 6-7). The news affects Paul strongly: "Now we live, if you are standing fast in the Lord" (v 8). He gives thanks to God and continues to pray for them (v 9-10).

These verses are filled with joy as Paul expresses his deep love for the Thessalonians and his commitment to them. He longs to see them again and prays that God might make that possible (v 11-13). Delighted though he is that his sufferings have not filled them with doubt, Paul is not satisfied: he is aware that there is knowledge they lack (v 10) and longs for them to increase and abound in love (v 12). Once again we see that Paul's goal is to see these Christians standing ever more firm in their faith.

OPTIONAL EXTRA
As an extra prayer activity, find some information about persecuted Christians around the world and spend some time praying for them as a group.

GUIDANCE FOR QUESTIONS
1. What is some good news you have received recently? This question is designed to get everyone talking and to introduce the theme of good news, which will come up later in the study.

2. What did Paul do, and what was his purpose in this (v 1-2)? Paul sent Timothy to Thessalonica to exhort the Thessalonian believers and establish them in their faith—in other words, to strengthen them in their knowledge of the truth and to encourage them to live out their faith.

3. What does Paul want the Thessalonians to know about the afflictions he is experiencing (v 3-4)? Paul says suffering was "destined" to come (v 3). He warned the Thessalonians that it would happen. It is not a surprise.

• **Why might hearing about these afflictions have affected the Thessalonians' faith?** Suffering, whether our own or other people's, can knock our faith off track. This is what Paul means by being "moved by these afflictions" (v 3). It can stop us from trusting in God's good plan and purposes. But Paul wants the Thessalonians to realize that God always works for our eternal good. God knew about the afflictions Paul would experience; they are not evidence that God is failing or is untrustworthy.

4. What news has Timothy brought (v 6)? Timothy has reported to Paul that the Thessalonians are doing well spiritually, are continuing with the Lord, and are established in faith and love. He has also said that they have not lost their love for Paul but are eager to see him.
Note: The word Paul uses for "good news" in verse 6 is usually used for the good news of the gospel message. This is actually the only time that Paul calls anything that is not the announcement of the gospel of Jesus Christ "good news"! So this is extravagant language that Paul is choosing to use.

5. Why do you think this news affected Paul so strongly (v 7-8)?
- The "faith and love" described by Timothy in verse 6 sums up the whole of the Christian life. We trust in Jesus, and we love him and each other. So it's no wonder that Paul is so excited. The Thessalonians are not just vaguely going on in their faith in a half-hearted way. They are fully committed and growing in their faith. All Paul's prayers have been answered.
- Paul has described himself as a parent to the Thessalonians. We see his deep love for them again here as he says, "For now we live, if you are standing fast in the Lord" (v 8). Paul loves these believers like his own children; he is fully emotionally invested in them. That's why he has been so comforted.

EXPLORE MORE
Read 1 Thessalonians 2:19-20
How does Paul describe the Thessalonians here? They are his "hope or joy or crown of boasting before [the] Lord Jesus," his "glory and joy." In other words,

they are the reward he is looking forward to in heaven; they are what he boasts about.

6. APPLY: Paul's dearest concern is that the believers will stand firm in their faith. If that were our dearest concern too, how would it affect...
- **what we say to each other?** Even when we are talking with other believers, we are not always thinking about how to build up one another in faith. Could we be like Timothy—aiming to "establish and exhort" others in faith?

- **what we invest time and energy in?** Paul is an example to us in how committed he was to building up the faith of others. What would it look like for us to invest more of our emotional energy and our time into supporting those around us—whether that's by teaching, evangelism, practical help, pastoral care, or something else?

7. What do you think is the tone of these verses overall? These verses are marked by rejoicing and by confidence in all that God can do. Paul uses superlatives—"all the joy", "most earnestly", "abound in love".

8. How does Paul express his joy in verses 9-10? Paul says he could not give enough thanks for the Thessalonian believers. He gives thanks not just for some joy but for "all the joy" that he feels! This joy also translates into a deep commitment to prayer. It fuels Paul to keep on praying night and day.

9. What does Paul continue to pray for (v 10-13)?
- Paul says twice more that he longs to see the Thessalonian Christians, asking God for an opportunity to see them face to face

(v 10) and praying that God will direct his way to them (v 11).

- Paul continues to pray for the Thessalonians' faith. He knows that certain things are lacking; they have had only a limited amount of teaching so far, and Paul wants to continue to instruct them. But this is not just about knowledge; it is also about how they live. Paul wants them to "increase and abound in love for one another" (v 12) and to "establish [their] hearts blameless in holiness" (v 13).

10. By "what is lacking in your faith" (v 10), Paul means teaching about the gospel. How do you think this links to the love and holiness Paul talks about in verses 12-13? Knowledge of God's word is supposed to transform us and help us to lead godly lives, because in God's word we

learn what is God's will. Paul was an apostle specifically equipped by God to explain the truth. For us today, the Bible is what supplies the truth to us; it's in the Scriptures that we have all the knowledge we need to grow in faith and love.

11. What is Paul ultimately looking forward to? Paul is looking forward to the return of the Lord Jesus.

12. APPLY: Can you think of specific individuals for whom you can pray some or all of Paul's words in verses 9-13? You might like to think of some of the following: church leaders; young people; new Christians; older saints; parents of young children; those training for leadership or attending theology courses.

4 1 Thessalonians 4
MORE AND MORE

THE BIG IDEA
Believing in Jesus impacts the details of the way we live—including our sexuality, our work, and the way we grieve. Let's encourage each other to look forward to his coming.

SUMMARY
Paul has already said he wants the Thessalonians to "walk in a manner worthy of God" (1 Thessalonians 2:12). In chapter 4 he gets specific.

First Paul reminds his readers of his previous instructions about sexual practices

(v 2-8). These verses help us understand why sexual immorality is such a problem: it arises from a lack of self-control and is a sin against fellow-Christians, as well as showing disregard for God. Paul also includes a warning about God's justified anger against those who turn away from him and commit sexual sin.

In verses 9-12 Paul talks about brotherly love. He commends the Thessalonians for their concern and care for one another and for other Christians (v 9-10)—evidence of God's work in their lives. He urges them to work hard and live quietly, not courting controversy or burdening others but living in such a way that nobody can accuse them of wrongdoing (v 11-12). All of this can be boiled down to two exhortations: please God and love one another.

In verses 13-18 Paul moves on from life now to life in the future—the second coming of Christ. The Thessalonians seem to be worrying about what happens to believers who die before Jesus returns. Paul assures them that there is hope. Just as we are confident that Jesus rose from the dead, so we can be confident that all believers will rise from the dead (v 14). Paul describes what God has revealed to him: Jesus will descend, the dead will rise, the living will be caught up with them in the air, and all of us will be with the Lord forever (v 16-17). This is the eternal future we are looking forward to—and it is the thought of this future that will encourage us to live the lives God has called us to in the meantime.

OPTIONAL EXTRA

To help you visualize what Paul is describing in verses 13-17, you could invite group members to draw it. They could produce a simple cartoon strip or, if they're more arty, they could spend a longer time painting or drawing the scene of Jesus' return.

GUIDANCE FOR QUESTIONS

1. What techniques do people use to get others to behave in a certain way? Which techniques do you think are most effective? In today's study, we will see Paul give instructions and encouragements to his readers. He seeks to motivate them by helping them to look to the future. This question is designed to introduce this theme. You might discuss various different situations (in the family, at work, in the political sphere) and various techniques: threats, rewards, persuasive words, and so on.

2. What is Paul's tone as he starts his instructions (v 1)?
- Paul is urging and imploring his readers. He is like a personal trainer, pushing Christians in order to help them to achieve their goal.
- He is also encouraging—affirming what they are already doing.
- He seeks to motivate and help them, reminding them that they can "please God" through what they do.
Note: The phrase "please God" is easily misunderstood. Pleasing God is not about earning God's approval. If we are in Christ, God already loves us. But it gives him pleasure when we walk in his way. It's like a child pleasing their father; God loves us and is eager to be pleased by us!

3. Paul's first set of instructions is about sexual immorality. What are the three points he makes in verses 3-6?
- Abstain from sexual immorality (v 3).
- Control your own body (v 4) instead of giving in to the passion of lust (v 5).
- Don't transgress and wrong your brother (i.e. fellow believers, v 6).

- **How do verses 3-8 help us to understand what sexual immorality is and why it is serious?**
  - Sexual immorality arises from a lack of self-control (v 4-5). Non-Christians may tell us to do whatever we feel like doing, but Christians are called to have control over our passions and lusts, rather than to be mastered by them. We get our marching orders from God's word, not from how we feel at a given moment.
  - Sexual immorality means wronging other believers (v 6). (See the Explore More section for more on this.)
  - Sexual immorality is sinning against God (v 7, 8). It is disregarding God's call to holiness, which is disregarding

God himself. This deservedly brings God's anger. (This does not mean that sexual sin cannot be forgiven—nor does it mean that true believers will never struggle with these things. But we must never make peace with sexual sin or seek to justify it.)

EXPLORE MORE
Read Romans 12:4-5 and 1 Corinthians 6:17-20
What do these passages tell us about our relationship with each other and our relationship with Christ? We are joined to the Lord (1 Corinthians 6:17), and this is not just as individuals—we are "members of one another" (Romans 12:5).
According to 1 Corinthians 6, why is sexual immorality sinning against God? Our bodies are temples of the Holy Spirit; we belong to God. So if we misuse our bodies, we are misusing what is his.
Given what we saw in Romans 12, why is sexual immorality therefore sinning against our brothers and sisters? Just as we are united to Christ, so we are united to our brothers and sisters through faith, like one body. This means that if one member sins, it hurts us all.

4. Paul says that knowing God makes Christians more able to control their bodies than the Gentiles (v 4-5). What does Paul say about God that helps and motivates us (v 3, 6, 7-8)?
- Verse 3 says that God's will is our sanctification. Sanctification means growing in godliness. Godly living is what God wants for us.
- Verse 7 explains this further. "God has not called us for impurity, but in holiness." We are saved by the blood of Jesus, but God's work in us does not stop there: we are called into a life of holiness.

- In other words, because we have been saved, we have the capacity to live a life of growing godliness. If God has called us into something, it means he will help us with it. Sanctification is something God works in us to achieve.
- Verse 8 reminds us of how God works sanctification in us: by his Holy Spirit. If we turn away from pursuing a life of holiness, we are disregarding the Spirit's work in us.
- Verse 6 tells us that this leads to God's justified anger. So there is a negative reason to obey as well as a positive one— we are being "solemnly warned" about the consequences of turning away from God and committing sexual sin.

5. What observations does Paul make about the believers' love for one another in verses 9-10? Paul encourages the believers: they are already showing brotherly love, not only to each other but also to all the Christians in Macedonia (v 9). But he doesn't just say what a great job the Thessalonians are doing. He also says they have been "taught by God" (v 9). Their love for each other is evidence of God's work in their lives.

6. Why does Paul give the instructions in verse 11? What do you think each of them means?
- Living quietly means not courting attention or controversy.
- Minding your own affairs means living wisely in such a way that you don't burden other people unnecessarily.
- Paul's instruction to "work with your hands" doesn't mean that manual labor is more godly than an office job; the emphasis is on working hard to support yourself, if you can.
- The point of all this is to "walk properly before outsiders." Nobody should be

able to accuse Christians of wrongdoing. We are not to make life harder for one another or for anyone else. Working hard and minding your own affairs are a way of showing brotherly love—and so they commend the gospel to those around us. **Note:** Paul is not saying we shouldn't allow our brothers and sisters to love and look after us. The phrase "be dependent on no one" cannot mean "cut yourself off from others" or "get through life on your own," because these things would contradict the exhortation to show brotherly love in verses 9-10. What Paul is saying is *Don't burden others unnecessarily.*

7. APPLY: Overall in this passage, what kind of people does Paul want us to become? Practically, what can we do to become more like this? 4:1-12 can be boiled down to two exhortations: please God more and more, and love one another more and more. We are to consciously reject living self-focused lives and instead live for God and for one another. This means being self-controlled, godly, hard-working and full of compassion.

8. What is the practical purpose of what Paul writes here (v 13)?
Paul writes to comfort the believers. He wants to help them to face death with hope. They will still grieve when they lose loved ones, but they will not be without hope.

9. What are the two key truths in verse 14 that bring us hope?
• Jesus has risen again.
• So will we!

• **Why is Paul so confident of these truths (v 15)?** He has a "word from the Lord"; he is speaking with the authority that God has given him as an apostle.

10. Use the following questions to help you trace out the various steps Paul describes in verses 16-17.
• **What will Jesus do (v 16)?** Jesus will descend from heaven with a cry of command.

• **Who will rise first (v 16)?** Then those who have already died will rise—they will be given new bodies.

• **What will happen next (v 17)?** Those who are alive at the time of Jesus' coming will be gathered to Jesus too.

• **What is the eternal future we're looking forward to (v 17)?** This is the greatest comfort of all: "We will always be with the Lord." We are looking forward to a real, physical eternity in which we will be with Jesus forever.

11. Why do you think these things should encourage us (v 18)? Even as we face death, we can find comfort and strength as we realize that we will always be with the Lord—nobody and nothing can take that away from us—and that we will one day be reunited with our loved ones who died trusting that same Lord.

12. APPLY: How do you think it changes our approach to life now if we believe these truths about the future?
• It changes the way we deal with hard things. There is always hope, even in the darkest times.

• It motivates us to pursue the things of God now—since those are the things that will last. So we will grow in godliness and say no to sin.

• It helps us to trust the Lord in times of fear. We will always be safe with him; he has a plan stretching into eternity. That means we can trust him and not be afraid.

5 1 Thessalonians 5
CHILDREN OF LIGHT

THE BIG IDEA
We are called to live in readiness for Jesus' return—and to do so together. Let's love each other and love God.

SUMMARY
Paul now tackles his key theme of the return of Christ head-on (v 1-11). He warns his readers that the second coming will happen unexpectedly, like a thief in the night. But this need not scare us. Paul remind us that we are "children of light": we have seen the light of salvation in Christ and are safe with him (v 5, 9-10). Using a metaphor about drunkenness and sobriety, Paul urges us to live in line with our identity as saved children of light, rather than acting in an immoral way like children of darkness, who are ignorant of God (v 4-8). He tells us to "put on" the armor of faith, love, and hope, which we have been given in Christ.

In light of this, Paul then offers some concluding words on how we are to pursue godliness as a church. We are to respect our leaders, be at peace with one another, warn those who are disobeying God, and help and encourage those who are weak or doubting (v 12-15). We are to rejoice, pray, give thanks, and listen to God's word (v 16-21).

Paul's big closing prayer is that God will sanctify us—cause us to grow in holiness (v 23-24)—and it is clear that every church member has a part to play in that. Yet Paul reminds his readers that it is God who does this work of sanctification. And God is faithful. As we seek to please him, we can trust him to continue to transform our lives.

OPTIONAL EXTRA
To illustrate Paul's metaphor about darkness and light, try turning the light off (unexpectedly if you like!) partway through the study and invite the group to keep reading. If it's dark enough, they won't be able to! The point is that it's great to be children of light—we can see the truth, get to know God better, and understand the right way to live, unlike those who are in the darkness of ignorance about God.

GUIDANCE FOR QUESTIONS
1. What do people today think might bring about the end of the world as we know it? When people believe these things, how does it affect the way they live now? Here are two sample answers:
- Many people are very worried about climate change. This might lead to small lifestyle changes—they recycle more or eat less meat. Or it might cause bigger changes—they avoid particular careers or engage in protests. In a more general sense, it can cause people to be continually anxious about the future of the world.
- Some people worry about wars and the collapse of civilization. This might cause them to be particularly anxious about politics, spending lots of time watching the news or, again, engaging in demonstrations. Or they may devote time or money to humanitarian causes.

2. Why doesn't Paul need to write about the "times and seasons" of Jesus' return (v 1-2)? They already know that it will come "like a thief in the night"—i.e. unexpectedly.

3. What do you think the metaphor about labor pains tells us about the day of Jesus' return?
- It's definitely coming, just as a pregnant woman will definitely give birth.
- It's going to come suddenly and will be impossible to predict exactly.
- It's going to be painful—for unbelievers.

4. We can't know when it will happen—but Paul says that it doesn't have to be an *unpleasant* surprise (v 4). What is it that means we can be safe when Jesus returns (v 5, 8-10)?
- We are not in darkness—we are "children of light" (v 5). In other words, we have seen the light of salvation in Christ.
- We have the "breastplate of faith and love, and for a helmet the hope of salvation" (v 8). A breastplate and helmet protect soldiers. When we put our faith in Jesus, love God and others, and hope in salvation, we will be protected from the painful aspects of Jesus' return.
- God has destined us for salvation through Jesus Christ—which means that nothing can pluck us out of his hand. We are safe!

5. What are Paul's specific instructions (v 6-11)?
- He urges us to keep awake and be sober (v 6).
- He tells us to "put on" the armor of faith, love, and hope, which we have been given in Christ (v 8).
- He instructs us to encourage one another and build one another up in faith (v 11).

6. APPLY: In what areas of life is it tempting to lack self-control and therefore live in line with the darkness?
The metaphor of sobriety is a helpful one. It points to being self-controlled—using the things of this world in moderation, rather than focusing solely on them. This applies to many different parts of life: our alcohol and food consumption; our sexual practices; our attitude to work, careers, and money; the way we conduct ourselves in conversation… You can probably think of lots more!

- **How can we "encourage one another and build one another up" in these situations?** Go back to the specific situations you've discussed already and think about how a Christian brother or sister might be able to help someone in that situation. You could also discuss more general ways in which we encourage one another as Christians—through attending church and Bible-study groups together, through praying for one another, through sharing verses or thoughts that will lift our eyes to the Lord, and so on.

7. How would you sum up the attitude Paul wants us to have to each other (v 12-15)? We should have an attitude of love (v 13, 14, 15); of respect (v 12); and of peace and unity (v 13, 14).

8. How would you sum up Paul's big prayer for the Thessalonians (v 23-24)? Paul prays that God would sanctify us—cause us to grow in holiness.

9. What role does each of the following people play in the sanctification of the believers?
- **Church leaders (v 12)** Church leaders labor for, lead, and admonish the believers. "Admonish" speaks of the pastor's or elder's work in reminding others of what they know and what impact it should have in their lives. So it's effectively another way of saying "teach." Church leaders are there to actively guide and teach their congregations, helping them to know what is right.

- **All Christians in a church (v 13-15)**
  - We are to respect, esteem, and love our leaders, acknowledging their authority over us so that we can grow under their guidance.
  - We are to be at peace with one another—being committed to one another so that everyone can focus on God.
  - We are to actively help one another to grow in faith. We should warn those who are out of line; we should encourage and strengthen those who are fainthearted and give aid to those who are weak; we should be patient with one another. In other words, we are to be concerned about one another's spiritual well-being and engage with one another about important things in the Christian life.
- **God himself (v 19-20, 24)** God guides us by his Spirit (v 19-20)—see the Explore More section for more on this. Ultimately it is God who works sanctification in us (v 24). When we seek him, we will grow more like him.

EXPLORE MORE
Read Acts 17:10-11
How did the Bereans test Paul's prophetic words? They examined the Scriptures to make sure that what he was saying was in line with what God had already revealed in his word.
Read Acts 24:24-25
In what sense do you think Felix was quenching the Spirit? It seems as if the Spirit was bringing about some sort of conviction in Felix's heart—but he was scared. He put off listening to the word of God.
How might we do something similar today, even as Christians? We might ignore a conviction of sin that the Spirit has brought about within us—refusing to repent even though we know we should. We might disobey God intentionally. We might fail to read his word or ignore it when we do read it.

10. Look at the commands in verses 16-22. How might each of these help us to live in the light of Jesus' return?
- Verses 16-18 have to do with prayer. We are to rejoice, pray, and give thanks. These things do not always come naturally! But Paul urges us to do them because they remind us that God is at hand and at work. We can always trust that he is working for our good (Romans 8:28). Rejoicing, praying, and giving thanks will help us to trust God even in the hardest situations and to look forward to Jesus' ultimate return.
- Verses 19-22 have to do with the Spirit. Commentators disagree on what "prophecies" means here and whether prophecy happens today, but what is clear is that the Spirit is always at work to build God's church and help us to live in line with God's will. This is why Paul immediately tells us to "hold fast what is good" (v 21). The Spirit will reveal to us what is good and help us to abstain from evil (v 22).

11. How does Paul's prayer in verses 23-24 help us as we seek to grow in godliness? Paul encourages us to see that sanctification is the work of God in us. He doesn't say, *May God aid you as you sanctify yourselves.* He says, "May the God of peace himself sanctify you completely." God is far more committed to and far more active in achieving our sanctification than we are. And so we can be confident that one day we really will be completely blameless and perfect before Christ. We can't reach perfection in this life, but when

Jesus returns, all our sins will be taken away. Having this confidence spurs us on to trustfully pursue godliness now.

12. APPLY: Which of the various commands here do you think your church or your group could particularly grow in? Read back through verses 12-28 together and discuss which ones apply best to you. Try to be practical and think of examples of what you're talking about.

---

2 Thessalonians 1
FAITH IN AFFLICTION

THE BIG IDEA
God is powerful and just—and this is never clearer than when we are suffering. When we meet with opposition or affliction, let's give thanks and ask for more of God's power in us.

SUMMARY
Paul starts this letter with thanksgiving, noting the love, steadfastness, and faith of the Thessalonian church (v 3-4). It becomes clear that the Thessalonians are facing persecution, and this is the main theme of the first chapter of the letter.

Paul explains that the Thessalonians' suffering is actually evidence of the righteous judgment of God. One reason is that their steadfastness in the face of it proves that their faith is really real, so God will be right to save them (v 5). Another reason is that these afflictions show that God's anger against sinners is just (v 6). The persecutors deserve to be punished, and they will be.

Paul therefore encourages his readers to see that, when Jesus comes again, those who are afflicting them will indeed be punished (v 7-9), while those who have believed in him will be given relief (v 7) and a place in glory with Jesus (v 9). One day we will marvel at Jesus' glory and strength (v 10), and this is a reason to believe in the Bible's testimony about Jesus—the only way to be saved.

The chapter finishes with a description of Paul's prayer asking that God will continue to make the Thessalonians worthy of his calling and to fulfill their resolve for good. This is an enormous encouragement to those who are suffering: we can look forward to glory and know that the Lord is by our side in the meantime.

OPTIONAL EXTRA
Here is a quick game to illustrate the fact that we need God's power in order to endure suffering. Divide the group into two teams and give both teams two sheets of newspaper and some tape. Then give one team a hardback Bible or something else fairly solid and heavy. Both teams have five minutes to make a 12in (30cm) tower plus some projectiles, just using these materials. Each team will then try to knock over the other team's tower by throwing their projectiles. The tower with the Bible in it should survive better—illustrating how God strengthens us. (Or, if the team with the Bible choose to use that as a projectile, the

game will illustrate how God will ultimately destroy all those who oppose him.)

GUIDANCE FOR QUESTIONS

1. Can you think of some times when people have opposed your faith? What happened? How did you respond? Encourage a few group members to share their stories. It could be something very simple, like being mocked or teased for your faith—or something more serious.

2. Why do you think Paul starts with thanksgiving (v 3-4)? Paul is about to talk about the difficulties the Thessalonian church is facing. But Paul knows that thanksgiving is important. It's key to fighting discontentment. Paul wants to encourage the Thessalonians by highlighting all that God is doing among them before he gets into discussing the difficult things they are facing.

3. What is currently happening to the Thessalonians, and how are they responding (v 4)? They are being persecuted but are responding with steadfast faith and perseverance.

4. One reason is given in verse 5. What does this situation tell us about the Thessalonian Christians? (See also verse 4.) They are "worthy of the kingdom of God" (v 5). In other words, they are responding to suffering with "steadfastness and faith" (v 4)—showing that their faith is really real.

- **Why might suffering actually be a good thing for them, therefore?** Suffering is a strength test for the Thessalonians' faith—and it is making them more steadfast. It is also an opportunity for them to see how much God has changed them and is guarding

their faith. They can rejoice knowing that they are safe in him.

EXPLORE MORE
Read Acts 5:41 and Philippians 1:29
What view of persecution is given here? How does this contrast with our usual view of suffering? These early Christians viewed suffering for Christ as a gift. We are worried that we might suffer for Jesus' sake, but the earliest Christians would have been worried if they had not!
Read 1 Peter 1:6-7
What is good about suffering in this instance? Peter says that persevering in trials is a sign that our faith is genuine. Knowing this brings great joy; we can praise God for guarding our faith!

5. Another reason why persecution is evidence of God's righteous judgment is given in verses 6-10. What does Paul tell us about the persecutors (v 6, 8)? They are afflicting the Christians because they do not know God and do not obey the gospel.

- **Why is God right to punish them, therefore?** They have chosen to ignore God and worship something else. It seems that they have heard the gospel and refused to listen to it, rejecting Jesus' offer of forgiveness. Refusing to believe the gospel carries eternal consequences.

6. APPLY: How might this understanding of God's righteous judgment influence the way we respond to unjust and sinful behavior? God punishes injustice; we can be confident that what is contrary to God's word is going to be punished. This both frees us and spurs us on. It frees us because we know that all wrongdoing will be avenged; we don't need to do it. It spurs us on because we have clarity about what is right and wrong; we can stand up to injustice. At the same time, we should also be aware that we ourselves are sinners; we are only saved by God's grace. So when others act sinfully, we should be seeking to respond with grace and to introduce them to Jesus if we can.

- **What do verses 3-4 suggest we could pray in response to suffering?**
  - We can give thanks—Paul says we "ought always" to do so! Thanking God for his work in us and in others will keep us focused on him and help us not to despair at what is going wrong.
  - We can pray for growth in faith, love, and steadfastness in those who are suffering.

7. What does Paul say will happen to the persecutors when Jesus returns (v 8-9)? Jesus will inflict vengeance on them for their wrongdoing. They will suffer "eternal destruction."

8. What's the key thing the persecutors will miss out on (v 9)? They will be kept away from the presence of the Lord and his glory.

9. What does Paul say will happen to those who have been persecuted, meanwhile (v 7, 10)—and why?
- God will grant them "relief" from their afflictions (v 7).
- They will marvel at Jesus and be together with him (v 10).
- All this is because they have believed Paul's testimony about Jesus (v 10).

10. How does this illustrate what we have seen already about how God distinguishes between people to punish and people to save? It is people's response to the good news of the gospel that determines what will happen to them on the day of judgment.

11. APPLY: How does this passage encourage us to stick to our resolve when we encounter those who oppose the gospel?
- It helps us to be confident in where we are heading.
- It helps us to be confident that God will deal with those who are opposing us.
- It helps us to be confident that the gospel of Christ really is the only way to be saved.

12. APPLY: How might praying a prayer like the one mentioned in verses 11-12 help us to be confident as we face suffering? Resolve is a work of God in our lives. He is the one who makes us worthy of his calling. When we depend on him, we can be confident that he will help us.

7 2 Thessalonians 2
LET NO ONE DECEIVE YOU

THE BIG IDEA

False teaching can bring us fears about the future and shake our confidence. But God is powerful and sovereign. Let's cling to the truth about him.

SUMMARY

Paul is concerned that the Thessalonians may be being disturbed by false teaching about Jesus' second coming (v 1-2). Not wanting their faith to be unsettled, he writes about what will happen before and after Jesus returns (v 3-12).

The "man of lawlessness" (v 3) is a mysterious figure who will appear before Jesus returns. He will come from Satan (v 9) and oppose every object of worship, setting himself up in God's place (v 4). He will seek to deceive people, and all those who have rejected the truth will follow him and believe what is false (v 10-12).

All this may sound unnerving, but Paul's key point is that God remains in control. The man of lawlessness is currently being restrained (v 6-7), and ultimately he will be destroyed (v 8). We can avoid being taken in by him simply by loving the truth about Jesus that has already been revealed to us.

Paul reminds his readers of several things that are true of all believers: they are beloved, chosen, and called by God, and destined for glory (v 13-14). It is by having confidence in these truths that the believers will stand firm in their faith (v 15).

At the end of a chapter filled with danger, Paul closes with a prayer of blessing (v 16-17). We need it!

OPTIONAL EXTRA

As a lighthearted introduction to the idea of deception and truth, play the game Two Truths and a Lie. Each person must come up with two true statements and one lie about themselves. Everyone else has to vote on which they think is the lie. The winner is the person who correctly identifies the most lies. You could use this in conjunction with questions 5-7 to help you discuss how to stick to God's truth and avoid Satan's deceptions.

GUIDANCE FOR QUESTIONS

1. Can you think of some things that might shake people's faith, causing them to doubt or to disobey God? This is an introductory question to get the group warmed up—don't spend too long on it. One answer might be that when someone's life doesn't go to plan or they suffer, they start to doubt that God cares. Another answer is false teaching: when someone has been taught wrong expectations about the Christian life, it will shake their faith when those expectations aren't met. Or when they have a shaky grasp of what Scripture really means, they may be easily led astray into other ways of thinking. Jealousy of others' lifestyles, lack of self-control, and fear for the future can all play a part in shaking people's faith.

2. Why is Paul writing this passage (v 1-2)? Paul doesn't want his readers to be shaken up and upset in their thinking. Clearly they have some concerns and questions about the future return of Jesus. In fact, some of them are afraid that the day of the Lord has already come and they've missed it! Paul is pastorally concerned—he doesn't want their faith to be unsettled.

3. What does he [the man of lawlessness] do (v 4)? He seeks worship.
He opposes every object of worship, including false gods—and, more importantly, he also opposes the true God, setting himself up in his place.

- **What is going to happen to him (v 8)?** He will be revealed, and then Jesus will come and utterly destroy him—not with a sword, not with fire, but with a mere breath of his mouth.

- **What's happening to him right now (v 6)?** He is being restrained. It's unclear who or what is doing this! It is possible that Paul means that the rule of government has a restraining influence on lawlessness. But whether the restrainer is a principle or an individual, it is clear that the main point is that God is in control. Whoever or whatever this restrainer of evil is, God simply uses him or it to operate through.

- **Who sends him (v 9)?** He comes from Satan.

EXPLORE MORE
Read Daniel 8:24-25
What points of similarity can you spot with the passage in 2 Thessalonians?
- This figure's power is not his own—just as the power of the man of lawlessness comes "by the activity of Satan" (2 Thessalonians 2:9).
- He will be full of deceit and many people will be taken in by him, leading to their destruction (see 2 Thessalonians 2:10).
- He will rise up against other figures of greatness.
- He will ultimately be destroyed "by no

human hand"—which fits with the idea that Jesus will destroy him "with the breath of his mouth" (2 Thessalonians 2:8).

Why is this passage ultimately one of comfort? This powerful figure will be destroyed. We can be completely confident of that.

4. Many people will be deluded by this "man of lawlessness." Who are these people—what have they already done (v 10, 12)? They have already refused to believe in the gospel.
- **How do they come to be deluded (v 10-12)?** They start off by refusing to believe the truth. God then confirms them in their delusion and allows them to be led off into error by the man of lawlessness.

5. How can we avoid being deluded or deceived ourselves, therefore? By believing and loving the truth about Jesus.

6. APPLY: How do we do this? What does it look like in our daily lives to love the truth? God's word is our defense. If we want to avoid being deceived by claims that stand in opposition to Jesus, we must know, remember, and stand on the word of God. This means being in church every Sunday, and reading the Bible on other days too!

7. APPLY: All of this doesn't just apply to the end times. In what ways might we be tempted to worship the wrong thing or give in to Satan's deceptions? How can we stand against this? We may idolize beauty, talent, health, wealth, sexual satisfaction, or many other things. We may think that we can solve all our problems on our own, or put our hope in other humans to do that for us. Satan wants

to undermine our worship of God and lead us into disobedience. The clearer we are on the truth and the more committed we are to obeying God's word, the more easily we will be able to stand against this.

8. In verses 13-14 Paul reminds his readers of several things which are true of all believers. What are they?
- Christians are "beloved by the Lord"—and nothing can change that.
- Christians have been chosen by God. Ephesians 1:4-5 tells us that God chose us before the foundation of the world. (This suggests that the best rendering of this passage is "chose you from the beginning" rather than "chose you as the firstfruits," as the ESV has it.) We did not choose God; he chose us (see John 15:16), before we had done anything to deserve the choice.
- Christians are being sanctified by the Holy Spirit. In other words, God is at work in us to make us more godly.
- Christians have been called by God to obtain the glory of Jesus. We are looking forward to an end point: one day we will see Jesus face to face and be with him in the place of perfect righteousness, where we will make our home.

9. In the light of what we read in verses 1-12, why do these truths give us comfort and hope? If it depended on us to keep on standing firm in the truth and not be deceived, we would be right to be alarmed by all that Paul says about the man of lawlessness! But it depends on the unchanging God. Nothing can change the facts: he chose us, he loves us, he is working within us, he has called us, and he is preparing us for a place of glory. We can trust him.

10. Why do you think this chapter closes with Paul writing a prayer of benediction (v 16-17)? This chapter has been filled with many dangers, toils, and snares! Paul has given answers to the Thessalonians' questions, but some of those answers must have generated some fear. This is why Paul pronounces a blessing on them—and us—at this point. We need it!

11. How does the past inform what Paul prays for the future here? Paul has complete confidence in God's comfort and grace, based on what Jesus did on the cross. We can have "eternal comfort" because God's gift of salvation is "through grace," which means it doesn't depend on anything we can do, and therefore it lasts forever. This is why Paul is able to confidently ask Jesus and the Father to comfort his readers' hearts and establish them in every good work and word. The way God has already cared for them is proof that he will continue to care for them.

12. APPLY: Why might verses 13-17 be helpful for someone who is...
- **afraid about something in the future or something happening now?** These verses will remind them that God has chosen and called them (v 13-14). His comfort is eternal (v 16); he is always by their side, no matter what happens. Based on verses 16-17, we might pray for comfort and hope for such people.

- **doubtful and uneasy about the end times?** These verses will remind them that what Jesus has already done is a guarantee of what he will continue to do (v 16). Verse 15 will urge them to stand firm in their beliefs even when it is hard; they are not the first person to doubt! Verse 14 will remind them of what they are looking forward to: the glory of our Lord Jesus

Christ, which will be worth the wait. Based on verses 16-17, we might pray that such people will be established in every good work and word.

- **being attracted by false teaching?**
  These verses will urge them to stand firm in the truth; they can trust what they read in Scripture (v 15). Based on verses 16-17, we might pray that God will establish such people in the truth and remind them that the hope they have in Jesus is a good and true hope.

8 2 Thessalonians 3
DO NOT GROW WEARY

THE BIG IDEA
Being confident in God means we will pray for each other and we will deal carefully with sinners. Let's prayerfully seek unity and encourage each other.

SUMMARY
Paul's confidence in God is clear at the start of 2 Thessalonians 3. He asks for prayer for himself (v 1-2) and prays for the Thessalonians (v 5) on the basis that God is faithful (v 3-4); he will establish their faith, despite the opposition they are facing.

Then it is as if Paul has read back through his letter and thought of a few more instructions he wants to add!

He has heard about some members of the Thessalonian church who are refusing to work and becoming busybodies instead (v 6, 11). Paul tells them that this is not right—recalling his own hard work among the Thessalonians and encouraging them not to burden one another unnecessarily (v 7-12).

Paul is concerned that the other believers may grow weary of doing good, presumably out of frustration at the idleness of these few individuals (v 13). So this issue is important. Paul is very clear that Christians should not condone, approve of, or enable those who are not doing good (v 14). In fact, they shouldn't even associate with those who are openly doing wrong. Yet this does not mean that wrongdoers should be cut off altogether. Paul reminds us that they are brothers, not enemies (v 15). We should always be willing to seek and celebrate repentance and reconciliation. In light of this, Paul prays for peace among the Thessalonian Christians (v 16).

This chapter helps us to understand what it should look like to be the church—encouraging and praying for one another, taking sin seriously, caring for one another as brothers and sisters, doing good, and following Jesus' commands. All this with the help of our faithful Lord!

OPTIONAL EXTRA
To help you put Paul's prayers into practice yourselves, you could print out a list of all your church's members or of all its ministries

and groups. Then set up stations around the room with different labels, using phrases from the passage. For example:

- That the word of the Lord may speed ahead and be honored.
- That we may be delivered from wicked and evil men.
- May the Lord direct your hearts to the love of God and to the steadfastness of Christ.
- Do not grow weary in doing good.
- May the Lord of peace himself give you peace at all times in every way.

Divide up your list of names between group members, and then invite everyone to circulate around the different stations, praying for the people on their list in light of the key phrase at each station. If you like, you could provide sticky notes and pens so that people can write down their prayers.

GUIDANCE FOR QUESTIONS

1. What things might give people either confidence or a lack of confidence in how to pray for others? Encourage the group to be honest about their own feelings as well as just talking in abstract terms. In this session we will see some examples of how to pray for one another, which may help those who feel less confident in knowing what to pray.

2. What does Paul ask for prayer for (v 1-2)? He asks his readers to pray for the spread of the gospel and for the success of the gospel (v 1), and for deliverance from opponents who were hindering his ministry.

3. What does he suggest *he* is praying for (v 5)? Paul asks the Lord to help the Thessalonians know the love of God and the steadfastness of Christ. In other words, he wants them to remember the truth that God loves them and to look squarely at the endurance of Jesus Christ for us.

4. How does Paul show his confidence in God throughout these verses—despite the opposition?

- Paul doesn't start his requests with the "wicked and evil men"—he begins by asking for prayer that the word of God will "speed ahead" (v 1). He is focused on what God can do, not on his fears of opposition.
- Paul doesn't simply pray that the word of God will go out and be heard; his language is much more positive than that. (He seems to have Psalm 147:15 in mind: "[God] sends out his command to the earth; his word runs swiftly".)
- Paul's statement that "the Lord is faithful" (2 Thessalonians 2:3) is utterly confident. He doesn't need to defend what he is saying—he just knows it is true!
- Paul promises that God "*will* establish you and guard you against the evil one" (v 3, my emphasis). He doesn't say "might" or "may".
- Paul sees that, with the Lord's help, the Thessalonian Christians are already doing the things he has commanded (v 4). God is working in them and will continue to do so.

5. Why will focusing on the love of God and the steadfastness of Christ help the Thessalonians (and us) to have confidence too? When we are being called to endure difficult things, we can look at Jesus' steadfastness for us. He endured poverty, suffering, pain, sorrow, rejection, mocking, torture, and death for us. He is able to empathize with us in the things we have to endure. And he loves us; he is faithful in establishing and guarding us. So whatever forces are ranged against us, keeping Jesus' steadfastness and God's love in mind will mean we can endure with faith and obedience intact.

6. APPLY: Who could you pray both of these things for? Try to think of specific examples. You might discuss church leaders and staff, missionaries, and church planters; you might talk about individuals who are facing opposition for standing up for their faith at work, or others who are having to endure difficult things.

7. What behavior has Paul heard about in the Thessalonian church (v 6, 10-11)? Idleness. They are refusing to work and becoming busybodies instead!

- **How does this contrast with Paul's own attitude to work (v 7-8)?** Paul was not idle! Despite the pressures and demands of his gospel work, he and his companions worked night and day to earn their own bread. He did not want to burden anyone unnecessarily.

8. But what does Paul say they ought to be doing and why?
- They should "do their work quietly and … earn their own living" (v 12).
- This is a matter of obedience—to Paul (v 10) and to the Lord Jesus himself (v 12).
- It will mean that they won't be a burden on others unnecessarily (v 8; see 1 Thessalonians 4:9-12).
- Note that Paul is not talking about those who are unable to work. He is addressing those who could work but are refusing to.

9. Why might the idleness of some believers have caused others to "grow weary in doing good" (v 13)? They're frustrated. We can so easily grow weary of doing the right thing when there are people around us—in our own congregation even—who are not living in accord with the Bible. It sows the thought, "Why bother?"

EXPLORE MORE
Read 1 Corinthians 12:21-27
What point about our relationship to each other does this metaphor help us to grasp (v 25-26)? We need to care for one another. A body can't be divided—and it should be the same with Christians. We should work together for one another's good and for God's kingdom.
Why does idleness threaten our relationships as Christians? Someone who is idle is effectively saying that they are more important than the other body parts. They are refusing to play their own role and asking others to work twice as hard. This is not how a body is supposed to work and can only lead to division.
Why does a lack of generosity to each other also threaten our relationships as Christians? Abandoning Christians who are needy would be like an eye saying to a hand, "I have no need of you." Again, it is not how a body is supposed to work—every member is equally important, regardless of how impressive or unimpressive they seem.

10. What attitude does Paul want Christians to have toward believers who are being disobedient (v 14-15)?
- They should not condone, approve of, or enable those who are not doing good.
- They shouldn't even associate with those who openly do wrong. This shows them that disobedience to God's commands is not just a different way of living as a Christian; it is wrong, and it is serious.
- Yet this does not mean these wrongdoers should be cut off altogether. Paul says they are not enemies but brothers (v 15). They may be acting in a way that is not in line with God's word, but Paul still wants to win them back. We should always be willing to seek and celebrate repentance and reconciliation.

11. Paul prays for God's peace "at all times in every way" (v 16). What kinds of peace might this congregation need?

- Peace within their hearts, as they fear opposition.
- Peace between each other, as they tackle sin and conflict within the church.
- Peace with God—now, as they seek to live in a godly way, and in the future, when they stand before the throne of judgment.

12. APPLY: How does this chapter as a whole help us to understand what it should look like to be the church?

- We pray for each other.
- We encourage each other to have confidence in the Lord.
- We share the word of God and pray for it to "speed ahead and be honored" (v 1).
- We love each other without becoming burdens on each other unnecessarily.
- We imitate godly leaders and follow Jesus' commands.
- We do good.
- We are brothers and sisters—and this means we seek to help each other turn away from sin.

Dive deeper into
1 & 2 Thessalonians

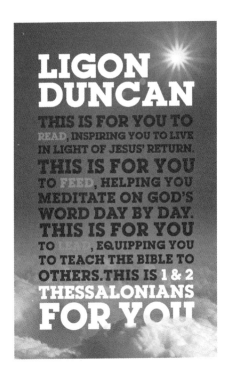

"Paul spends a lot of time in these two letters talking about the future—and in every chapter, we also see him showing how this future relates to our daily lives now. The fact is, you cannot live life well if you're not living it in light of Jesus' return."

Verse by verse, pastor Ligon Duncan unpacks the letters of 1 & 2 Thessalonians, helping us to apply them to our lives today. This accessible and absorbing expository guide can be used for personal devotions, alongside small-group studies, or for sermon preparation.

Good Book Guides
The full range

Galatians: 7 Studies
Timothy Keller

Ephesians: 10 Studies
Thabiti Anyabwile

Ephesians: 8 Studies
Richard Coekin

Philippians: 7 Studies
Steven J. Lawson

Colossians: 6 Studies
Mark Meynell

1 Thessalonians: 7 Studies
Mark Wallace

1&2 Thessalonians:
8 Studies
Ligon Duncan

1&2 Timothy: 7 Studies
Phillip Jensen

Titus: 5 Studies
Tim Chester

Hebrews: 8 studies
Michael J. Kruger

Hebrews: 8 Studies
Justin Buzzard

James: 6 Studies
Sam Allberry

1 Peter: 6 Studies
Juan R. Sanchez

2 Peter & Jude: 6 Studies
Miguel Núñez

1 John: 7 Studies
Nathan Buttery

Revelation: 7 Studies
Tim Chester

TOPICAL

Man of God: 10 Studies
Anthony Bewes & Sam
Allberry

Biblical Womanhood:
10 Studies
Sarah Collins

The Apostles' Creed:
10 Studies
Tim Chester

The Lord's Prayer:
7 Studies
Tim Chester

**Promises Kept: Bible
Overview:** 9 Studies
Carl Laferton

The Reformation Solas
6 Studies
Jason Helopoulos

Contentment: 6 Studies
Anne Woodcock

Women of Faith:
8 Studies
Mary Davis

Meeting Jesus: 8 Studies
Jenna Kavonic

Heaven: 6 Studies
Andy Telfer

Mission: 7 Studies
Alan Purser

Making Work Work:
8 Studies
Marcus Nodder

The Holy Spirit: 8 Studies
Pete & Anne Woodcock

Experiencing God:
6 Studies
Tim Chester

Real Prayer: 7 Studies
Anne Woodcock

Church: 8 Studies
Anne Woodcock

God's Word For You

Galatians For You

"The book of Galatians is dynamite. It is an explosion of joy and freedom which leaves us enjoying a life of blessing. I pray that it explodes in your heart as you read this book."

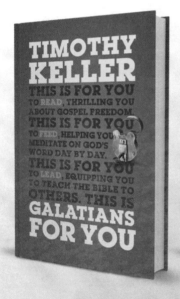

Daniel For You

"The book of Daniel offers you the knowledge that God is still at work, the confidence that it is possible to remain faithful to Jesus Christ, and the strength to live for him in our day."

Find out more about these resources at:

www.thegoodbook.com/for-you

BIBLICAL | RELEVANT | ACCESSIBLE

At The Good Book Company, we are dedicated to helping Christians and local churches grow. We believe that God's growth process always starts with hearing clearly what he has said to us through his timeless word—the Bible.

Ever since we opened our doors in 1991, we have been striving to produce Bible-based resources that bring glory to God. We have grown to become an international provider of user-friendly resources to the Christian community, with believers of all backgrounds and denominations using our books, Bible studies, devotionals, evangelistic resources, and DVD-based courses.

We want to equip ordinary Christians to live for Christ day by day, and churches to grow in their knowledge of God, their love for one another, and the effectiveness of their outreach.

Call us for a discussion of your needs or visit one of our local websites for more information on the resources and services we provide.

Your friends at The Good Book Company

thegoodbook.com | thegoodbook.co.uk
thegoodbook.com.au | thegoodbook.co.nz
thegoodbook.co.in